Every amazing mamma was once a new mom.
She said, "You are not alone." ♥

...Said The New Mom

by Emily Malaquias

Illustrated by Geo Aquino

This book is dedicated to my Mum, who was a teen mom and then had two sets of twins less than a year apart. Thank you for always figuring it out, rising above and most importantly teaching me the power of being sweet, kind and wonderful.

"No one ever told me about that..."

...Said the new mom

"I'm sorry to call again, but I'm just not sure...

Is this normal?"

...Said the new mom

"I hope my baby knows how hard I am trying."

...Said the new mom

"I'm thankful they brought lunch but, I would be so grateful if they helped with the dishes."

...Said the new mom

"Is this milk
or am I sweating?"

...Said the new mom

"I didn't know I would need so much care and recovery for so long..."

...Said the new mom

"I wish I had some cute PJs and comfy robes to wear around the house."

...Said the new mom

"Baby clothes with zippers, better yet two way zippers are the best!"

...Said the new mom

"Diapers and wipes are my favorite gifts."

...Said the new mom

"I love giving you a bath... when is the last time I washed my hair?"

...Said the new mom

"That first smile is magic."

...Said the new mom

"We are finally getting a routine."

...Said the new mom

"I am so blessed to have this baby and this baby is so lucky to have me."

...Said the new mom

"Being a mom is the greatest thing I have ever done."

The Mamma said.

Made in the USA
Middletown, DE
27 August 2021